Vol. 1

The Message of the Cross

Mystery Hidden before the Ages

The Message of the Cross

Vol. 1

Mystery Hidden before the Ages

1. God is "I AM WHO I AM" • 6
2. God is the Creator • 16
3. God is Omniscient and Omnipotent • 26
4. God is the Author of the Bible • 36
5. God Created Men • 46
6. God Cultivates Men • 56
7. Adam and Eve in the Garden of Eden • 66
8. Reason Why God Placed the Tree of the Knowledge of Good and Evil • 76
9. The Law of the Redemption of the Land • 86
10. Mystery Hidden before the Ages • 96
11. Qualifications of the Savior • 106
12. 'Jesus' and 'Jesus Christ' • 116

 New Jerusalem Movement Checklist

Reading: Book of John
Lord's Footsteps

1. Mystery of the Beginning • 14
2. True Light Came to the Earth • 24
3. Jesus is the Son of God • 34
4. Jesus Made Wine from Water • 44
5. Jesus Taught the Mystery of Being Born Again • 54
6. Jesus Preached the Gospel to a Samaritan Woman • 64
7. Jesus Healed a Sick Man Who Suffered for 38 Years • 74
8. Jesus Walked on the Water • 84
9. Jesus Promised to Send the Holy Spirit • 94
10. Jesus Forgave a Woman who Committed Adultery • 104
11. Jesus Healed a Blind Man • 114
12. Jesus is the Good Shepherd • 124

Introductory Remarks

The Message of the Cross is a mystery that God concealed a long time ago, namely, from the time before the beginning of the world. It is His hidden plan to save all men who were to be destined to Hell due to sins.

God created men to gain true children with whom He can share love forever in the beauty of Heaven. But, since Adam, the first man, sinned, all men had no choice but to go to Hell.

The God of love, who knows everything, prepared the way of salvation before the ages. And when the time came, He sent His only begotten Son to the earth and allowed Him to be crucified for our sins on our behalf.

However, on the third day from His death Jesus resurrected and became our Savior. In God's plan, anyone who believes in Jesus Christ can receive salvation and live in the everlasting Heaven happily forever. When we realize the providence of salvation embedded in the cross, we can feel God's love and possess true faith.

Introduction
Before attending a Bible study, you can check your Christian life and your thoughts.
After reading the cartoon, talk about your thoughts and feelings.
Now let's look at a few things.

Strong Children Armed with the Word
This part is an edition of *The Message of the Cross* so that children can understand it better. If you preview it before the formal study time, the Holy Spirit will give you more wisdom and faith.

Activity

You can review what you learn and practice the Word in this part of the study.

There are three steps in the 'activity': They are labeled by age groups as step 1, 2, and 3 (Pre-school Kindergarten and Elementary Grades 1st thru 3; and 4th thru 6th)

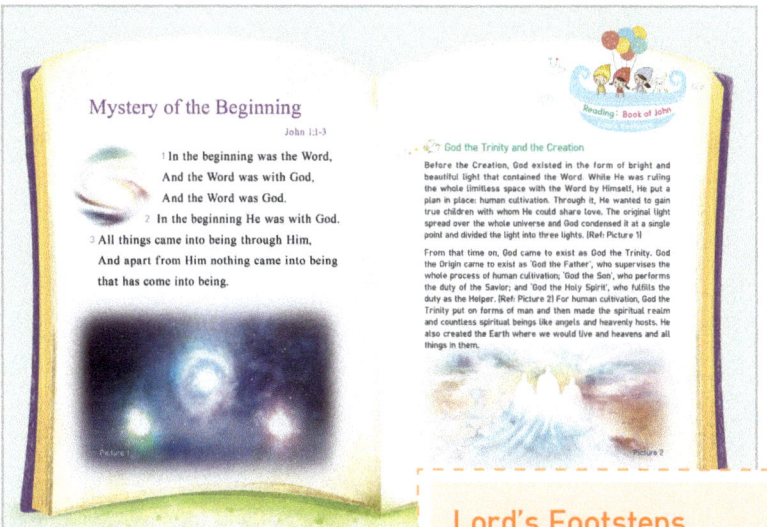

Lord's Footsteps

Reading the Book of John, let's follow the Lord's footsteps.

As you engrave the Lord's love, the spiritual meanings contained in the Book and results of this study on your hearts, your faith will grow rapidly.

God Is
I AM WHO I AM

Let's Read the Bible

"God said to Moses, 'I AM WHO I AM'; and He said, 'Thus you shall say to the sons of Israel, "I AM has sent me to you."'" (Exodus 3:14)

Let's Memorize Our Bible Verse

"In the beginning was the Word, and the Word was with God, and the Word was God." (John 1:1)

Family Tree

"Phew! It's so complicated."
"You're right."

"Your grandfather's grandfather's grandfather is... If you follow the family tree back up to the top, who do you think is there at the top? Do you know?"

"They are Adam and Eve. Adam and Eve are the ancestors of all mankind. They are the ones God created at the very beginning."

"Then, who gave birth to God who created Adam and Eve?"

Have you thought about who gave birth to God?

Strong Children Armed with the Word

We all have our own fathers and mothers. Due to them we could be born. Our parents also were born thanks to our grand-parents. When we back-date continually, at the top of our family tree are Adam and Eve whom God created and who are our first ancestors. Then, do you think God was born of His parents, or that He had been created by someone?

1. God the Creator is "I AM WHO I AM"

God made the heavens, earth, sea, moon, and stars as well as men. He also created every kind of animal like fish and birds and every kind of plant. So then, just how long has God existed? What did He look like at the very beginning?

In Exodus Chapter 3, God called Moses saying. "Moses, Moses!" He said to him, "I am the God of your father, the God of Abraham, the God of Isaac, and the God of Jacob." And He continued, "I will send you to Pharaoh, so that you may bring My people, the sons of Israel, out of Egypt."

Then, Moses said to God, "Behold, I am going to the sons of Israel, and I will say to them, 'The God of your fathers has sent me to you.' Now they may say to me, 'What is His name?' What shall I say to them?"

God answered him, "I AM WHO I AM". It means He is neither a being that someone gave birth to nor someone made. God is a perfect Being who has existed since before the beginning.

2. God the Origin existed in a form of light that contains sound

Reading the Bible very closely you can gain a clearer understanding about God I AM. 1 John 1:5 reads, "that God is Light, and in Him there is no darkness at all." This verse depicts the original form of God that is the Light. John 1:1 says, "In the beginning was the Word, and the Word was with God, and the Word was God." Here, it also says that God existed in the form of Word, which is the sound contained in the Light.

Have you ever seen the northern lights also called the Aurora Borealis? God created it for us to understand God's original form. 'In the beginning', God existed in just such a form. The Aurora can usually be observed in the Polar Regions. It varies in beautiful colors: red, blue, yellow, light green, and pink. As we have learned, God the Origin existed in the form of the beautiful and mysterious Light that contains clear and resonant sound, which is the Word. He was unimaginably beautiful light and sound and He controlled the whole limitless space as just Himself.

3. God the Trinity who put on a form of man

After a long period of time, God the Origin planned 'human cultivation' to gain true children who resemble Him. And as the first step in His plan, at one point, He condensed Himself the original Light, that had been spread boundlessly until then. God the Origin gathered the Light and proceeded into three Lights. Each of the Lights put on a specific form that was like a human form. Each of the three Lights had a face, a body, two arms, and two legs. From then, God the Origin began to exist in the form of God the Trinity. This is because for human cultivation God the Origin needed to exist in such a form as 'God the Father', who would supervise the entire process of human cultivation and raise men as His children who resemble Him; He needed to exist also as 'God the Son', who would fulfill the duty as the Savior; and also exist as 'God the Holy Spirit', who would work as the Helper. He prepared for it so that countless people would come to resemble Him in heart, and then enter the eternal Heaven and share joy and love with Him forever.

'The beginning': 'the beginning' that is recorded in John 1:1 is far earlier than 'the beginning' that is recorded in Genesis 1:1. This 'beginning' of Genesis 1:1, is in reference to the beginning of the Creation when the heavens and the earth were created.
Origin: The point from which (at which) something develops/ comes into existence
Cultivation: the planting, tending, improving, or harvesting of crops or plants

Step 1

● Color the fish below with aurora-colored pens.

Step 2

• Gather the letters in the maze below and fill in the boxes.

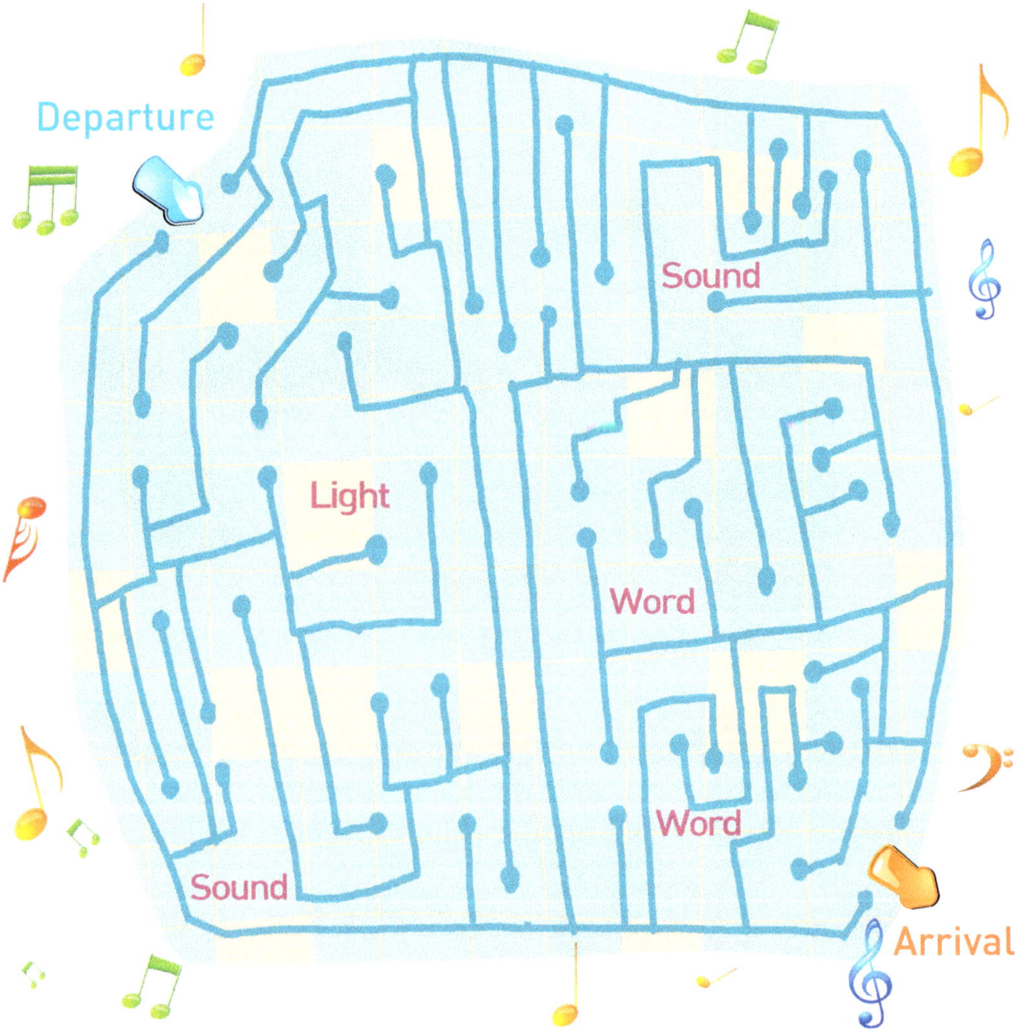

God exited in a form of [   ] that contained [   ], which is the [   ].

Step 3

- Read the following sentences and write the ones that are true/correct in the table below.

1 God is "I AM WHO I AM."

2 God was in a human form before eternity.

3 God existed only in a form of sound that is the Word.

4 God existed in a form of light that contains sound.

5 God existed in the form of light that contained noise.

6 "I AM WHO I AM" means God is a perfect Being who has existed as Himself since before eternity.

Write the numbers of the true/correct sentences.

- Write the two verses below using your Bibles.

John 1:1

 1 John 1:5

Mystery of the Beginning

John 1:1-3

1 In the beginning was the Word,
And the Word was with God,
And the Word was God.
2 In the beginning He was with God.
3 All things came into being through Him,
And apart from Him nothing came into being
that has come into being.

Picture 1

Reading: Book of John
Lord's Footsteps

God the Trinity and the Creation

Before the Creation, God existed in the form of bright and beautiful light that contained the Word. While He was ruling the whole limitless space with the Word by Himself, He put a plan in place: human cultivation. Through it, He wanted to gain true children with whom He could share love. The original light spread over the whole universe and God condensed it at a single point and divided the light into three lights. (Ref: Picture 1)

From that time on, God came to exist as God the Trinity. God the Origin came to exist as 'God the Father', who supervises the whole process of human cultivation; 'God the Son', who performs the duty of the Savior; and 'God the Holy Spirit', who fulfills the duty as the Helper. (Ref: Picture 2) For human cultivation, God the Trinity put on forms of man and then made the spiritual realm and countless spiritual beings like angels and heavenly hosts. He also created the Earth where we would live and heavens and all things in them.

Picture 2

God is the Creator

Let's Read the Bible

"By faith we understand that the worlds were prepared by the word of God, so that what is seen was not made out of things which are visible." (Hebrews 11:3)

Let's Memorize Our Bible Verse

"In the beginning God created the heavens and the earth." (Genesis 1:1)

Creation vs. Evolution

What do you think about evolutionism?

Strong Children Armed with the Word

There was someone who designed and built our houses. Even the pencil, there must be someone who made it. Then, how did the unimaginably big universe come to existence? It was created by God the Trinity—God the Father, God the Son, and God the Holy Spirit. He created the universe for us.

1. God created all the worlds by the Word

Genesis Chapter 1 tells us how God the Trinity created the heavens and the earth and all things in them. God created all of them with the Word. Not only the earth where we live but also the heavens, the sea, the sun, the moon, and stars and birds flying in the sky and fish in the sea were all created by Him. Every kind of plants and animals were created by His Word.

No matter how intelligent he is, man can't create something without material or ingredients. Though he has outstanding skill, if there is nothing to use, he can't make something. Only when he has materials, as wood or plastic, can he make a chair. Only when he has thread, needles, and fabric can he make a beautiful garment. But God the Creator who is the Almighty, created everything, without any existing materials. He did it just by the Word.

God didn't just make visible things like the heavens and the earth. But He also created the Garden of Eden where the first man, Adam, and Eve dwelt. He also brought about the heavenly kingdom, our eternal dwelling place.

2. The evidence showing that God is the only one Creator

On the earth are people of different races and they use different languages but their body structures are the same. For example, all of them each have two eyes, two ears, a nose, two nostrils, and a mouth. The location is also the same. The eyes are near the face's top, the nose is on its center, and the mouth is below the nose. And food goes into the mouth, passes through internal organs, and goes out of the body. This process also applies to all men.

Moreover, animals as well as men have the same facial structure and process

of digestion. If there had been several deities they would have formed men and animals just as they wanted. Then their appearances would have been different. One would have made several eyes, not two. Or the other would have made the facial structure different. But God is the only Creator and He designed and created everything, so all things have the same structure. By this fact, we can believe God the Creator. Thus, you must not worship false idols or bow before them.

3. God the Creator revealed in the nature

Romans 1:20 reads, "For since the creation of the world His invisible attributes, His eternal power and divine nature, have been clearly seen, being understood through what has been made, so that they are without excuse." Just as written, anyone can believe in God the Creator as long as they open their hearts.

The earth rotates once a day and revolves around the sun once a year. The moon rotates and revolves around the earth once a month. These cause day and night, the four seasons and ebb and flow of the tides. The distance between the sun and the earth is now the most appropriate. If the sun were closer to the earth than it is now, the earth would be too hot for men to live. If the sun were farther to the earth, the earth would be too cold. It is God who put them in the most proper place. Like this, God reveals Himself through the nature and leads us to the way of salvation and answers our prayers.

Worship: bow with respect

● Match the right pictures and draw lines to connect them

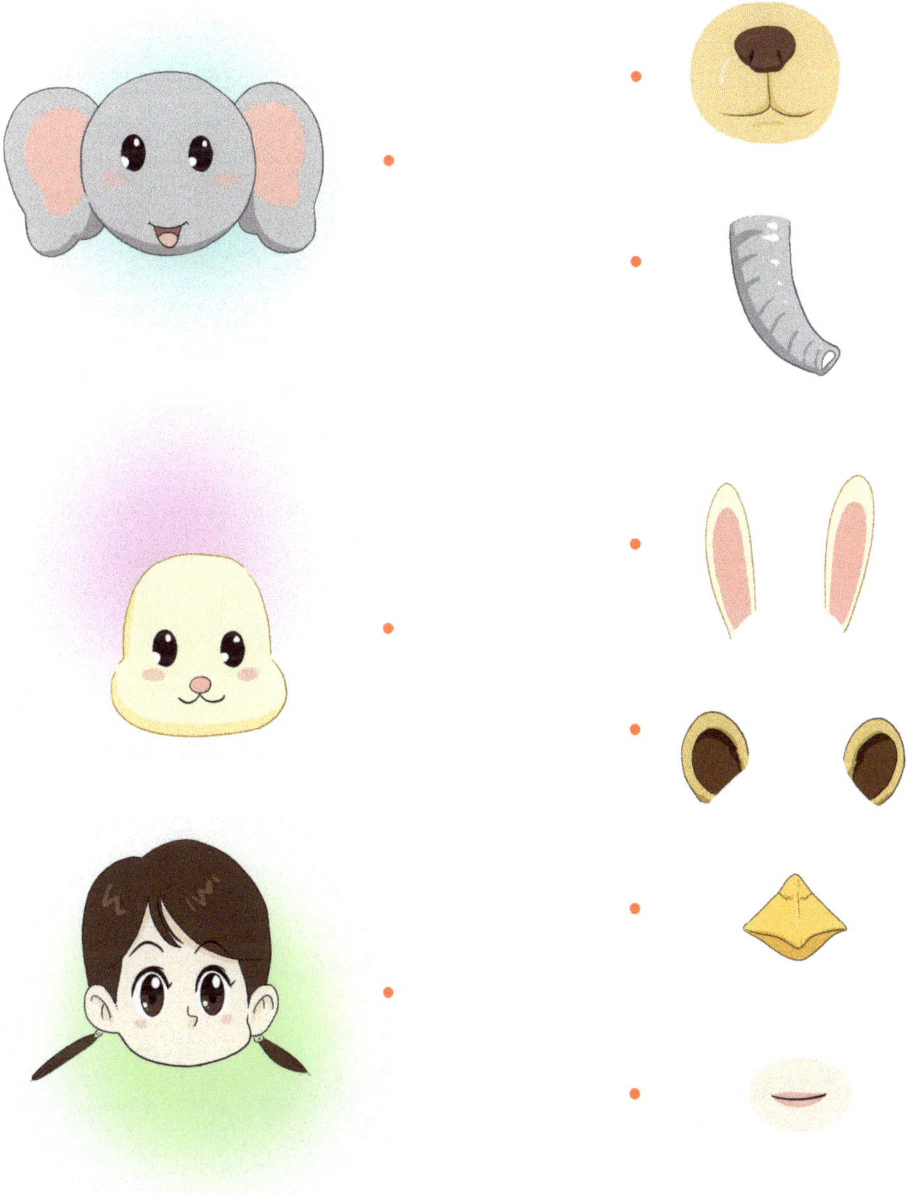

Step 2

● Countless people and animals have the same facial structure. It is just one of the proofs showing that there is one Creator. Find the images that are different from each other in the two pictures below (there are 7 different hidden images).

Step 3

- Look at the pictures below and write about the proof that God created the whole universe and all things in it.

- Read the passage below and fill in the blanks.

    For since the _____ of the world His invisible attributes, His eternal _____ and _____ nature, have been clearly seen, being understood through what has been _____ , so that they are without _____ . (Romans 1:20)

True Light Came to the Earth

John 1:9-12

9 There was the true Light which, coming into the world, enlightens every man.
10 He was in the world, and the world was made through Him, and the world did not know Him.
11 He came to His own, and those who were His own did not receive Him.
12 But as many as received Him, to them He gave the right to become children of God, even to those who believe in His name.

Picture 1

Jesus Christ and the Right to Become God's Child

Because Adam and Eve committed sin, their descendants all became sinners. They were destined to Hell. But the God of love sent the One to save them. It was God the Son. He came in flesh through the nation of Israel. He is Jesus. (Picture 1)

To fulfill His duty as the Savior, Jesus spread the gospel of the kingdom of Heaven and took the suffering of crucifixion and death for the sins of all mankind. On the third day from when He was buried, He overcame death and resurrected. By this, anyone who accepts Jesus Christ is able to be to be forgiven of all his or her sins and gain the right to become God's child. (Picture 2)

Picture 2

God is Omniscient and Omnipotent

Let's Read the Bible

"God was performing extraordinary miracles by the hands of Paul, so that handkerchiefs or aprons were even carried from his body to the sick, and the diseases left them and the evil spirits went out." (Acts 19:11-12)

Let's Memorize Our Bible Verse

"'I am the Alpha and the Omega,' says the Lord God, 'who is and who was and who is to come, the Almighty.'" (Revelation 1:8)

One Who Can Do Everything

Have you ever met God who is omniscient, knowing everything, and omnipotent, having all power?

Strong Children Armed with the Word

'God is omniscient and omnipotent' means that He knows everything and He can do everything. Children who believe this God will never feel sad even if they are faced with difficulties. This is because they believe God the Father knows all problems of His beloved children and He will resolve all of them.

1. God knows everything (He is omniscient).

God knows our hearts and minds as well as our deeds and words because He created us. He also knows what will happen in the future, so He recorded the history of humanity in the Bible. He recorded the birth of the Savior, the fall and restoration of Israel, things that will happen at the end time, and about Heaven and Hell. He let many things be written in it. Furthermore, He let the Word-abiding people who love God know what will happen in detail so that they can realize the depths of God's heart.

When we rely on God who knows everything, there is nothing impossible. You will be prosperous in everything and receive answers to whatever you ask.

2. To God, nothing is impossible.

The Bible tells us about countless amazing signs and wonders that couldn't have been done with human power and strength. If God the Creator is with us, we can see things created from nothing and people can receive answers by the prayer that transcends space and time. Nothing is impossible!

In the Old Testament time Moses parted the Red Sea. When he stretched out his hand with his staff over the sea, it parted (Exodus 14:21). When he struck a rock with his staff, water came out of it (Exodus 17:6) and he also changed bitter water into sweet water (Exodus 15:25). When Elijah prayed earnestly heavy rain came to the land where there had been no rain for three and a half years. He also revived the dead.

What about our Jesus? He revived Lazarus who had been already dead for four days. He also let the blind see and healed people with all kinds of diseases. He also

walked on the sea. When He rebuked the winds and waves they became calm.

Apostle Paul loved God fervently. He also did things that were impossible with human power alone. When handkerchiefs or aprons were carried from him and people laid them on the sick, diseases and evil spirits went out (Acts 19:11-12). The living God has performed such amazingly powerful works that can't be done with human power because He desires all men to be saved through such works.

3. You can meet God the Almighty even today

Dr. Jaerock Lee, Senior Pastor of Manmin Central Church, has been allowed by God to perform God's amazingly powerful works and spread the gospel throughout the world. He has healed all kinds of diseases that can't be cured with medicine. He has made the blind regain their sight. He has let the lame who came to him in wheelchairs get up and walk and jump. He has also revived the dead.

As recorded in the Bible, by letting Dr. Lee perform signs, wonders, marvelous things, and extraordinary miracles, God led innumerable people to His arms. Hebrews 13:8 says, "Jesus Christ is the same yesterday and today and forever." Just as said, when we believe Jesus Christ today, we can meet God the Almighty and receive answers to whatever we pray.

Transcend: to go above or beyond (a limit, expectation, etc.)
Sign: things that can't be done with men's power like regenerating dead cells or organs in the work of God the Almighty

Step 1

● Circle the words that are identical.

Strength	Story	Strong	String
Almighty	Omniscient	Omnipotent	Omnipresent
Prayer	Prayer	Player	Prey
Healing	Healer	Hearer	Hill

Step 2

- God's 'Being omniscient and omnipotent' means He knows everything and He can do everything.
  Let's learn the Latin words "omniscient" and "omnipotent."

omni	scient	omni	potent

- In the situation below, what would you say to him? Look for the right response in the Bible and write the verse and memorize it.

Step 3

- Write what the 'almightiness' of God means in your own words.

In the Old Testament time...

example God parted the Red Sea through Moses and let the Israelites cross the sea on the dry ground. (Exodus 14:15-22)

In the New Testament time

example Peter said to a lame man, "In the name of Jesus Christ the Nazarene--walk!" Then, he came to walk and jump. (Acts 3:1-10)

Today

example My friend once suffered from atopic dermatitis but she was healed after receiving prayer.

- Jesus said when anyone who has no evil believes in the power of God and prays, he or she can manifest the power of God. Write the following verse about His word.

John 14:12

Jesus, the Son of God

John 1:32-34

32 John testified saying, "I have seen the Spirit descending as a dove out of heaven, and He remained upon Him.

33 I did not recognize Him, but He who sent me to baptize in water said to me, "He upon whom you see the Spirit

John the Baptist and the Son of God

John the Baptist prepared for the way of Jesus. He preached in the wilderness of Judea saying, "Repent, for the kingdom of heaven is at hand." And he baptized people in the River Jordan. "As for me, I baptize you with water for repentance, but He who is coming after me is mightier than I, and I am not fit to remove His sandals; He will baptize you with the Holy Spirit and fire," said John. He made the way of the Lord straight. (Ref: Matthew Chapter 3)

God said to John, "He upon whom you see the Spirit descending and remaining upon Him, this is the One who baptizes in the Holy Spirit." When Jesus was in Galilee he went to John the Baptist and received the baptism of water from John in the Jordan River. When John saw the Spirit descending as a dove out of heaven and remain on Jesus, he testified that Jesus was the Son of God.

Reading: Book of John
Lord's Footsteps

descending and remaining upon Him, this is the One who baptizes in the Holy Spirit."

34 I myself have seen, and have testified that this is the Son of God.

God is the Author of the Bible

Let's Read the Bible

"Seek from the book of the LORD, and read: not one of these will be missing; none will lack its mate for His mouth has commanded, and His Spirit has gathered them." (Isaiah 34:16)

Let's Memorize Our Bible Verse

"All Scripture is inspired by God and profitable for teaching, for reproof, for correction, for training in righteousness." (2 Timothy 3:16)

Whose Letter Is This?

Why did Serom's uncle shed tears?

Strong Children Armed with the Word

Have you ever written to your friends or parents? If you write a letter with your heart it will move the receiver's heart no matter whether it is to apologize or just to say 'thank-you'.. The Bible is like a letter that contains God's heart who desires all men to be saved and to enter Heaven. Then, what kind of book is the Bible and how was it written?

1. The 66 books of the Bible written under the inspiration of the Holy Spirit

There are countless books in this world, but none of them gives us true life. But the Bible can give us true life and eternal life. It tells us in detail about God the Creator, Heaven, Hell, the way of blessing, the way of salvation, and causes and solutions of diseases.

The Bible consists of 66 books as a whole. There are 39 books in the Old Testament and 27 books in the New Testament. The Bible is the collection of books written by 34 people over a period of 1,600 years. What's amazing, the whole Bible never contradicts itself and has consistency as if it had been written by one person. How could it be possible? It is because the Holy Spirit who is the heart of God moved people's hearts and made them write the books of the Bible. That's why the author of the Bible is God.

2 Timothy 3:16 says, "All Scripture is inspired by God…" 2 Peter 1:21 reads, "For no prophecy was ever made by an act of human will, but men moved by the Holy Spirit spoke from God." In other words, the Bible is God's Word that was written by men who were inspired by the Holy Spirit and they wrote it according to God's will.

2. The Bible is God's letter of love that contains His promise and blessing

God is spirit so He is invisible to the human eyes. So He reveals Himself in various ways. One of them is the Bible. All the books of the Bible from Genesis

to Revelation hold God's promise and blessings.

Genesis, the first book, tells us about how God created the world and men and what kind of blessing He gave to them. The books of Matthew, Mark, Luke and John make a record of the ministry of Jesus who came as the Savior and the providence of salvation. The book of Revelation describes in detail what will happen in the future and the most beautiful dwelling place in Heaven, New Jerusalem.

In this way, the Bible is a letter of love that keeps God's heart and will and it teaches us how people can receive salvation with faith and enter Heaven.

3. God's Word in the Bible is all true

The Old Testament includes the record of prophecy about Jesus' birth, suffering, crucifixion, and resurrection on the third day (Isaiah 7:14). And this prophecy was fulfilled just as written around 700 years later (Matthew 1:23-25). About 2,000 years ago, Jesus came to the earth, which is an obvious fact. The calendar eras, B.C. and A.D., are based on Jesus' birth. It is also true that Jesus was resurrected. The women who followed Jesus, His disciples and many other people witnessed the resurrected Lord.

Besides, the Bible contains many prophesies and most of them have been fulfilled. The-not-yet-fulfilled passages are what will be fulfilled in the near future such as Jesus' coming in the air, the 'Rapture', the Seven-year Great Tribulation, Millennium Kingdom, and the Great White Throne Judgment. We should clearly understand that all the verses of the Bible are true and keep the Word in it by praying more earnestly.

B.C.: Before Christ
A.D.: Anno Domini (In the year of Lord)

Step 1

• Guess what I am.

1. You carry me to church on Sunday

2. God's Word is written in me.

3. I have the Old Testament and the New Testament.

4. You can achieve a white heart

and a beautiful heart when you keep this Word.

Step 2

● Match the right answers.

- How many books are there in the Old Testament? • • God

- Whose word is written in the Bible? • • 66 books

- How many books are there in the New Testament? • • 39 books

- How many books are there in the Bible as a whole? • • Revelation

- What is the name of the last book of the Bible? • • 27 books

● Fill in the blanks with the right answers.

Examples　Jesus　　the Old Testament
　　　　　　the New Testament　the Holy Spirit

The Bible was written by people that were inspired by _____. The Bible is divided into _____ and _____ with _____ birth as the dividing point.

Step 3

- The verses of the Bible have verses they pair up with. The prophecies in the Old Testament were fulfilled in the New Testament time. Let's find out the prophecies about Jesus and what has been fulfilled.

Around 700 years later

(Isaiah 7:14)

"Therefore the Lord Himself will give you a sign: Behold, a virgin will be with child and bear a ☐☐☐, and she will call His name Immanuel."

- Immanuel means 'God is with us'.

(Matthew 1:18-25)

Now the birth of Jesus Christ was as follows: Jesus' mother, Mary, was engaged to marry Joseph. But, before they came together she was found to be with child by the ☐☐ ☐☐ ☐☐☐ ☐☐☐ …but she was kept a virgin until she gave birth to a Son; and he called His name ☐☐☐ ☐☐.

Jesus Made Wine with Water

John 2:6-11

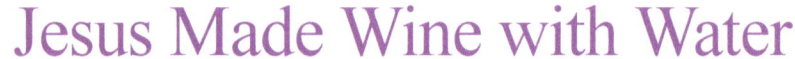

6 Now there were six stone waterpots set there
for the Jewish custom of purification, containing
twenty or thirty gallons each.
7 Jesus said to them, “Fill the waterpots with
water.” So they filled them up to the brim.
8 And He said to them, “Draw some out now and
take it to the headwaiter.” So they took it to him.
9 When the headwaiter tasted the water which had

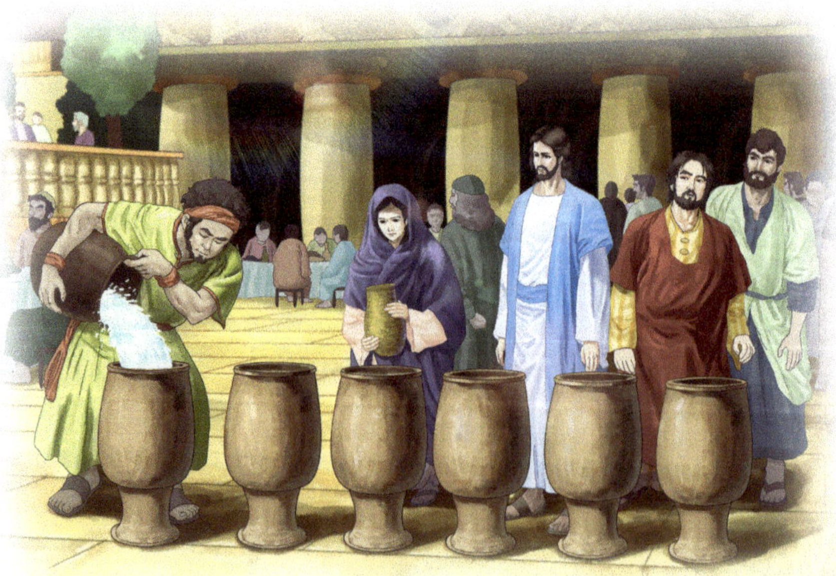

become wine, and did not know where it came from (but the servants who had drawn the water knew), the headwaiter called the bridegroom,

10 and said to him, "Every man serves the good wine first, and when the people have drunk freely, then he serves the poorer wine; but you have kept the good wine until now."

11 This beginning of His signs Jesus did in Cana of Galilee, and manifested His glory, and His disciples believed in Him.

Spiritual Meaning of Jesus' First Sign in His Public Ministry

The six stone waterpots symbolize the 6,000-year history of human cultivation that started when Adam committed sin and was driven to the earth. Jesus turned water into wine as the first sign after He began His public ministry. He let the people drink it, which carries deep spiritual meanings. It symbolizes Jesus would be crucified and would shed His precious blood when the appointed time came. It also meant that anyone who believes this will be forgiven of sins and reach salvation.

God Created Men

Let's Read the Bible

"God created man in His own image, in the image of God He created him; male and female He created them. God blessed them; and God said to them, 'Be fruitful and multiply, and fill the earth, and subdue it; and rule over the fish of the sea and over the birds of the sky and over every living thing that moves on the earth.'" (Genesis 1:27-28)

Let's Memorize Our Bible Verse

"By faith we understand that the worlds were prepared by the word of God, so that what is seen was not made out of things which are visible." (Hebrews 11:3)

The Mystery of Human Body

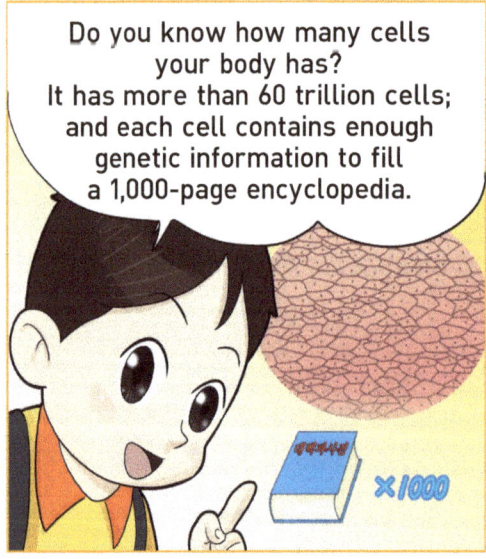

Among all our body parts God created, which one do you think is the most mysterious?

Strong Children Armed with the Word

Looking closely at our body, all parts from tiny cells to all internal organs are amazing. All things in the nature are all amazing. Then, how did God the Creator create the heavens, the earth, and all things in them and human beings?

1. God created the heavens and the earth and all things in them for six days

Hebrews 11:3 says, "By faith we understand that the worlds were prepared by the word of God, so that what is seen was not made out of things which are visible." God created the heavens and the earth by the word of God.

On the first day, when God said, "Let there be light," there was light, and separated the light from darkness; on the second day, the expanse that is heaven; on the third day, He divided the land and sea and made the grasses, the vegetation, and trees bearing fruit.

On the fourth day, He made the sun for the day and the moon and stars for the night. And on the fifth day, He created fish and the living things in the sea and birds flying in the sky. On the sixth day, He made livestock and creeping things and animals of the earth.

God made this suitable, beautiful environment for man to live and then He created man last. And He blessed him to subdue and rule over everything as written in Genesis 1:27-28.

2. God created men in His own image

How did God the Creator create man? He used dust from the ground as the ingredient. He formed man of dust from the ground in His own image. Here, the dust from the ground was soft and wet. After forming him of dust from the ground, He breathed into his nostril the breath of life. Then, he became a living being.

Here, the breath of life is the condensed crystal of all God's power. It is also God's strength or energy. It is the motive power that lets life be maintained. Adam

was the living being who was created in God's image. How gorgeous he was! Adam had clean and milky skin and he was well-built. From head to toe, he was beautiful.

3. When God breathed into his nostril the breath of life, Adam came to breathe and move.

The process of man's creation as the living being can be likened to the process of turning on a computer or TV. When we turn on a TV, various images appear on the screen. If you disassemble the TV, there are many lines and parts connected. God didn't just create the image of man of dust from the ground, but also He made all internal organs, bones, blood vessels, and nerve systems with His original light that is His power.

But before He breathed the breath of life into the man, he didn't move at all just like the TV that isn't plugged in without electrical current. After the breath of life that contains God's power came into his body, blood started to circulate and he came to breathe and move.

Just by seeing the brain of man, we can realize that it is complicated and it has limitless power such that it is called a 'small universe'. Innumerable scientists have studied the mystery of its ability, but what has been revealed about it is just a little part of its real ability. How incredibly amazing is God's power that created a men, all the heavens, the earth, and all things. It goes beyond our imaginations.

Strength: Your strength is the physical energy that you have, which gives you the ability to perform various actions, such as lifting or moving things.
Motive power: Any source of energy used to produce motion
Electrical current: electrical power

Step 1

- What things can we do with our bodies given to us by God? Match the right pictures and discuss with your friends what things are possible for you to do.

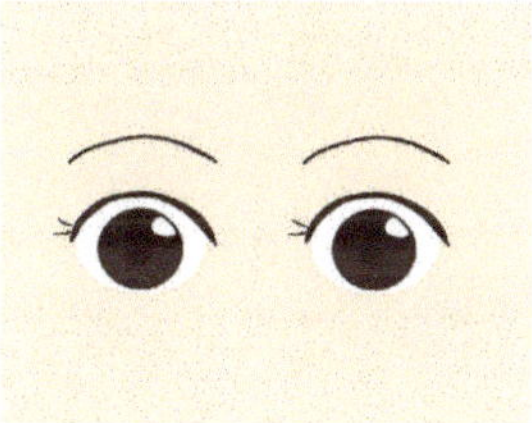

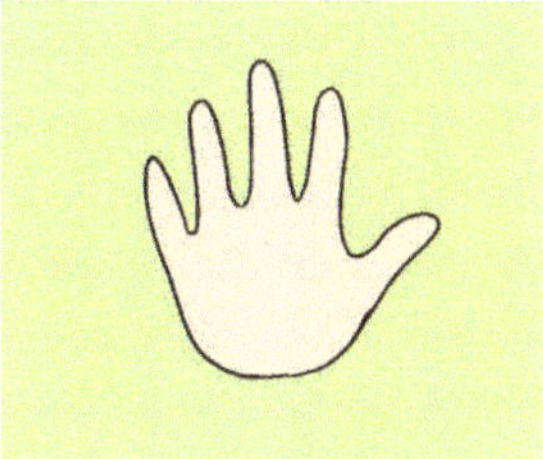

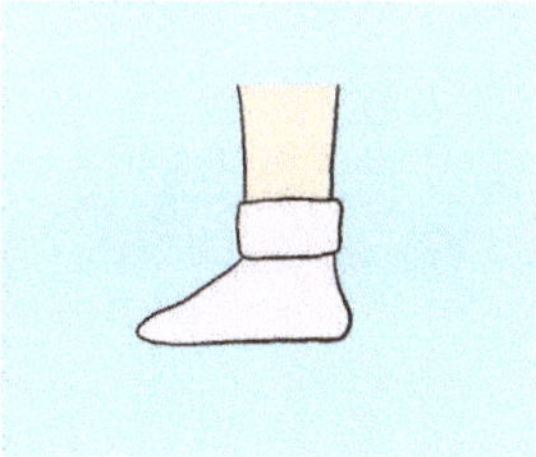

Step 2

- Looking at the pictures, put the numbers in the right order of the God's creation.

Sea and land

Light

Sun, moon, stars

Animals and man

Expanse (sky)

Fish and birds

Step 3

- Use the letters below and write the things that God created on the sixth day. You can use the letters as many times as you want.

For example   giraffe, man

_____

_____

- How did God create man? Use the Bible and fill in the blanks.

(Genesis 2:7)

"Then the LORD God formed _____ of _____ from the ground, and breathed into his _____ the breath of _____; and _____ became a _____ being."

Jesus Taught the Mystery of Being Born Again

John 3:1~5

1 Now there was a man of the Pharisees, named Nicodemus, a ruler of the Jews.

2 This man came to Jesus by night and said to Him, "Rabbi, we know that You have come from God as a teacher; for no one can do these signs that You do unless God is with him."

3 Jesus answered and said to him, "Truly, truly, I

Reading: Book of John
Lord's Footsteps

say to you, unless one is born again he cannot see the kingdom of God."

4 Nicodemus said to Him, "How can a man be born when he is old? He cannot enter a second time into his mother's womb and be born, can he?"

5 Jesus answered, "Truly, truly, I say to you, unless one is born of water and the Spirit he cannot enter into the kingdom of God."

What is 'being born again of water and the Spirit'?

To be born-again is to accept Jesus Christ, receive the Holy Spirit, and be born again as God's child. When you cast away hatred, jealousy, and greed according to the Word telling us not to do them and to throw them away, our hearts will be cleansed. When we love and serve others in accordance with the Word telling us to do and to keep something, our heart will be filled with the truth. The Holy Spirit helps us realize God's will and live according to God's Word.

 'Being born again of water and the Spirit' is to become men of the truth by the Word of God and the help of the Holy Spirit in that way. Only those who are born again of water and the Holy Spirit can enter Heaven as God's children.

God Cultivates Humans

Let's Read the Bible
"[God] desires all men to be saved and to come to the knowledge of the truth." (1 Timothy 2:4)

Let's Memorize Our Bible Verse
"His winnowing fork is in His hand, and He will thoroughly clear His threshing floor; and He will gather His wheat into the barn, but He will burn up the chaff with unquenchable fire." (Matthew 3:12)

Robot vs. Child

Why did the mother feel moved more by her daughter Jueun's song than the robot's song?

Strong Children Armed with the Word

Even if a robot obeys and it can do all things they want it to do, your parents love you more than the robot. They want you to realize their love and share love with them although you sometimes give them a hard time. It is the same with God who created men.

1. God wants true children who want to share love with Him

Your parents make many efforts to raise you. When you are sick, they can't sleep. They want to give you good things so they work diligently. Why do they give birth to and raise you though they knew they would have to do a lot of work to raise you? This is because they want to share love with you.

With such a heart, God made men and has cultivated them on the earth for a long time. 'Cultivation' is the process of sowing seeds, tending them, and bearing fruit. God lets men be born on this earth and has cultivated them because He wants to gain His true children who have a good and beautiful heart like His.

In Heaven, there are many angels that obey God's will like robots but they can't share love with God. What God really wants is true children who can share love forever and who please God with heartfelt obedience. That's why God made men and taught them His Word which is the truth. He has waited for a long time for us to become His true children.

2. There is no other choice but for the wheat and the chaff to be separated

Farmers sow seeds in the ground and farm with diligence so that they can reap a lot of fruit in the time of harvest. The seeds that are provided with proper nutrition become the 'wheat'. The others that aren't may become empty 'chaff'. Chaff is useless so it is used for fertilizer, or it is gathered and burned. As fall comes, farmers reap their fruit. In the same manner, God will finish the cultivation of humanity and He will gather the harvest when His appointed time

comes.

  God desires all men to be saved as wheat-like believers and to enter Heaven, but only one who does the will of God can enter. Matthew 3:12 reads, "His winnowing fork is in His hand, and He will thoroughly clear His threshing floor; and He will gather His wheat into the barn, but He will burn up the chaff with unquenchable fire." Here, 'wheat' stands for God's true children who achieve the hearts of goodness by living and acting according to the Word of God. On the other hand is the 'chaff' that refers to those who don't believe Jesus Christ, or who don't live by the Word even if they are believers.

3. Only 'wheat-like' believers can enter eternal Heaven.

  Heaven is a very beautiful and happy place. The glassy golden road, crystal clear waters of the River of Life, fascinating mansions decorated with gold and jewels… Their beauty can't be expressed with mere words. But Hell is a dreadful place where people will suffer in the Lake of Fire or the Lake of Brimstone.

  Then, why did God make not only the beautiful Heaven and but also Hell? This is because if there are evil men in Heaven where there are only love and goodness, the beauty of Heaven would become polluted with evil. Not everyone who accepts Jesus Christ and says to Him, "Lord, Lord" can enter Heaven. Only one who does the will of God can enter the beautiful Heaven and share love with God and enjoy the happiness forever.

The lake of fire and the lake of Brimstone: Unsaved souls will be thrown into the lake of fire or Brimstone after the Great White Throne Judgment of. The lake of Brimstone is the place where those souls who committed grave sins like speaking against, opposing, and disgracing the Holy Spirit. The lake of Brimstone is seven times hotter than the lake of fire.

Step 1

- **Choose and mark with circle children who live according to the Word.**

I help my mom.

I review the Bible study book.

I follow the latest pop songs.

I pray.

I offer worship service with a right attitude.

I am irritated.

Step 2

- **In pictures below, find out wheat and chaff and match relevant things.**

- **What about you? Are you like wheat or chaff?
What do you have to do to become like 'wheat' believers?**

Step 3

- What are some of the differences between robots, angels, and us? Why does God cultivate humans on the earth?

Difference

The reason why God cultivates mankind

- Write Matthew 3:12.

Jesus Preached the Gospel to a Samaritan Woman

John 4:7-10

7 There came a woman of Samaria to draw water. Jesus said to her, "Give Me a drink."

8 For His disciples had gone away into the city to buy food.

9 Therefore the Samaritan woman said to Him, "How is it that You, being a Jew, ask me for a drink since I am a Samaritan woman?" (For Jews have no dealings with Samaritans.)

10 Jesus answered and said to her, "If you knew the gift of God, and who it is who says to you, 'Give Me a drink,' you would have asked Him, and He would have given you living water."

A Samaritan Woman and the Water of Eternal Life

In the time of Jesus, Jews didn't speak with Samaritans because they hated and despised them. But Jesus went to Samaria and told a Samaritan woman who came to draw water to give Him water. He started a Samaritan conversation with her to preach the gospel to her. 'Water' spiritually means the Word of God. Just as men can live only when they drink water, we need to 'drink' the Word of God delivered by Jesus, namely, the water of eternal life to go the way to the eternal life. He wanted to let her realize this. This is the way that Jesus with His love, preached the gospel even to the Samaritan people.

Adam and Eve in the Garden of Eden

Let's Read the Bible

"Then the LORD God took the man and put him into the garden of Eden to cultivate it and keep it. The LORD God commanded the man, saying, 'From any tree of the garden you may eat freely; but from the tree of the knowledge of good and evil you shall not eat, for in the day that you eat from it you will surely die.'" (Genesis 2:15-17)

Let's Memorize Our Bible Verse

"Put on the full armor of God, so that you will be able to stand firm against the schemes of the devil." (Ephesians 6:11)

 # Difference

What is the difference between the two?

Strong Children Armed with the Word

Do you keep your parents' word in your heart? If you don't love them, you will forget their words and won't keep them either. But if you love them, you will keep their words and do what they told you to do. Likewise, if you love God you can keep His word in your heart and live by it, then you can receive His love and blessings.

1. Adam lived in the Garden of Eden for a long time

God created the Garden of Eden and put Adam in it. At first when Adam was created, he had no knowledge in his brain like a new-born baby. God taught him goodness, truth, and knowledge on the spiritual world and let him govern the Garden of Eden.

And He made Eve for Adam and gave her to him as his helper and blessed them to be fruitful and multiply. They lived in the Garden of Eden for an unimaginably long time and gave birth to countless descendants there. God let the first man Adam and Eve enjoy whatever they wanted in this place of abundance –the Garden of Eden. But God forbade them from doing one thing; they were not to eat from the tree of the knowledge of good and evil.

2. Adam committed the sin of disobedience

Adam and Eve kept the Word of God for a long time while living in the Garden of Eden. But as time passed, they failed to bear God's Word in their minds. The enemy Satan didn't miss the chance. Satan tempted Eve through a crafty serpent. The serpent said to Eve, "Indeed, has God said, 'You shall not eat from any tree of the garden'?" How do you think Eve responded to it?

In fact, God had clearly said, "But from the tree of the knowledge of good and evil you shall not eat, for in the day that you eat from it you will surely die" (Genesis 2:17). But Eve said in reply to it, "God has said, 'You shall not eat from it or touch it, or you will die.'" This sentence misses the word 'surely' and indicates that she may die or not. That Eve answered with a different sentence from what God had said is a proof of her not believing and bearing the Word of God in her mind.

Satan instilled greed into her mind saying she would become like God if she ate the fruit. From then, the fruit of the tree of the knowledge of good and evil looked good for food and desirable to make one wise to her. In the end, Eve ate from the tree of the knowledge of good and evil and gave it to her husband, Adam. He also ate it. What do you think happened to Adam and Eve who committed the sin of disobedience to the Word of God?

3. By the sin of one man, all men reached death

Adam was a living being before committing the sin and he could communicate with God. But his spirit became dead by violating God's command. Eventually, Adam and Eve were driven out of the Garden of Eden. At that time, the suffering of mankind was to begin. Adam's descendants were destined to fall into eternal death, that is, Hell because they inherited sins from Adam who disobeyed. Moreover, all animals and plants on the earth also came under the curse together with them.

In particular, the serpent that had tempted Eve was cursed more than all cattle and they came to go on their belly and eat dust all the days of their lives. In a spiritual sense, the serpents refer to the enemy devil and Satan. And the dust symbolizes men who were created from dust. Thus, serpents' eating dust means that Satan considers men who are living in sins their prey and brings tests, trials, and disasters to them. So if we commit sins we will become Satan's prey. So it's very important to remember the Word of God and act according to it.

Helper: A helper is a person who helps another person or group with a job they are doing.
Be fruitful: Something that is fruitful produces good and useful results.
Multiply: When something multiplies or when you multiply it, it increases greatly in number or amount.
Communicate: If you communicate with someone, you share or exchange information with them, for example by speaking, writing, or using equipment. You can also say that two people communicate.

Step 1

- Children who love God don't do what He tells them not to do. Why don't we go to the beautiful Heaven together with our friends?

Step 2

- Underline the different part between the two sentences: one is God's Word and the other is the Eve's word.

> God: "But from the tree of the knowledge of good and evil you shall not eat, for in the day that you eat from it you will surely die." (Genesis 2:17)

> Eve: "But from the fruit of the tree which is in the middle of the garden, God has said, 'You shall not eat from it or touch it, or you will die.'" (Genesis 3:3)

- Why did Eve change the Word of God?

- No matter how hard the enemy Satan tempts us, we should drive him away with the Word of God and achieve a victory. Find Ephesians 6:13 and write it down.

Step 3

● Write down the spiritual meanings of the words below.

- Serpent
- Dust
- The serpent's eating of the dust

● Just like the enemy Satan tempted Eve through the serpent, people around you sometimes tempt you to fall into sins. But if you arm yourself with the Word of God, you will win easily. Discover the Bible verse.

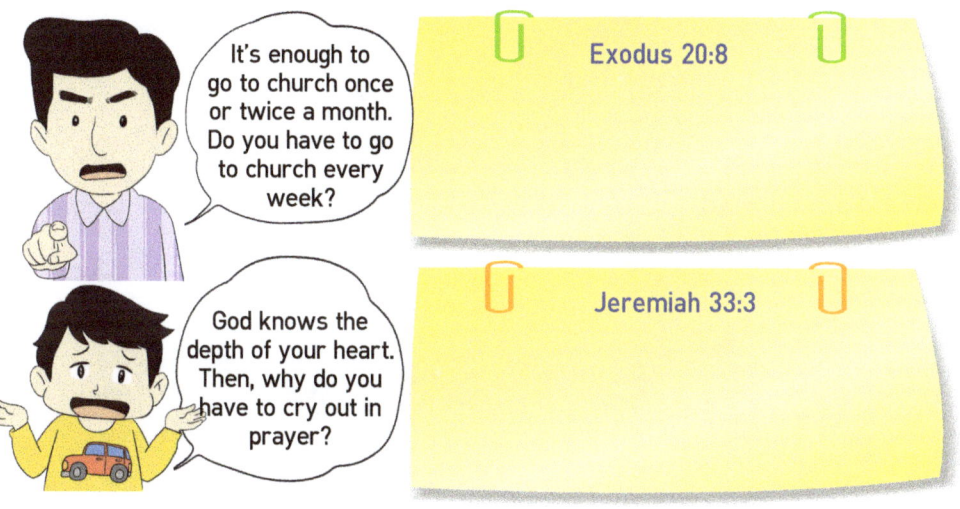

Jesus Healed a Sick Man Who Suffered for 38 Years

John 5:2-14

2 Now there is in Jerusalem by the sheep gate a pool, which is called in Hebrew Bethesda, having five porticoes.

5 A man was there who had been ill for thirty-eight years.

Reading: Book of John
Lord's Footsteps

6 When Jesus saw him lying there and knew that he had already been a long time in that condition, He said to him, "Do you wish to get well?"

8 Jesus said to him, "Get up, pick up your pallet and walk."

9 Immediately the man became well, and picked up his pallet and began to walk. Now it was the Sabbath on that day.

14 Afterward Jesus found him in the temple and said to him, "Behold, you have become well; do not sin anymore, so that nothing worse happens to you."

The Reason why Jesus Told Him Not to Sin Anymore

Jesus healed a man who had been sick for 38 years by a pool named Bethesda. Afterwards, Jesus found him in the temple again and said to him, "Behold, you have become well; do not sin anymore, so that nothing worse happens to you." Sins are the causes of diseases. Jesus wanted him to enjoy the blessing of good health by not sinning anymore and living according to the Word only.

The Reason Why God Placed the Tree of the Knowledge of Good and Evil

Let's Read the Bible

"The LORD God planted a garden toward the east, in Eden; and there He placed the man whom He had formed. Out of the ground the LORD God caused to grow every tree that is pleasing to the sight and good for food; the tree of life also in the midst of the garden, and the tree of the knowledge of good and evil." (Genesis 2:8-9)

Let's Memorize Our Bible Verse

"For I consider that the sufferings of this present time are not worthy to be compared with the glory that is to be revealed to us." (Romans 8:18)

Difference of Their Grateful Hearts

What is the reason why the two respond in different ways?

Strong Children Armed with the Word

There are children who feel happy and are thankful for a gift. Some others aren't happy and show no thankfulness when they receive a gift. Which one is lovelier to their parents? Of course, the former children who feel the love of the parents are lovelier. Adam, the first man, and Eve didn't feel happy and give thanks even though they lived in abundance in the beautiful Garden of Eden that God created for them. Why is that?

1. God placed the tree of the knowledge of good and evil in His providence to let people realize relativity.

It was not because He wanted people to eat from it and fall into destruction that God placed the tree of the knowledge of good and evil in the Garden of Eden. He put it there because it was His amazing providence that would later allow for people to experience the concept of relativity. Adam and Eve lived their lives lacking nothing, but they still could not feel thankfulness, joyfulness, and happiness. They didn't feel love. This is because they hadn't experienced the concept of relativity between things or situations.

In this world, there are many relative things. If you want to know the true value of an emotion or feeling, you need to know and experience the opposite of it. For example, those who have never lived in poverty don't know how good it is to live in affluence. This is because, though they have seen others' difficulties they haven't experienced poverty themselves. Also, those who haven't been sick don't know how great a blessing it is to enjoy good health. So they can't give thanks from the bottom of the heart. Likewise, only when we know hatred can we understand how good love is. Only when we have felt unhappy can we feel the value of happiness.

Adam and Eve had never experienced hatred, sorrow, pain, poverty, and diseases, so they didn't know how good everything was that they were enjoying. They didn't know and so they could not give thanks to God.

2. After experiencing the relativity, they felt true happiness

What if men live forever being unable to feel happy? What is the meaning of the life? Even though they have to suffer from something, if they can feel true happiness after all sufferings are gone, it will be much better. That's why God put the tree of the knowledge of good and evil in the Garden of Eden and He didn't stop Adam from eating from it by his own free will.

What happened to Adam and Even after they violated the Word of God and ate from the tree of the knowledge of good and evil? Just as God said, "You will surely die" their spirits, that were their masters, died. And they couldn't live in the Garden of Eden which is the spiritual world anymore and they were driven out from it. From then, they experienced tears, sorrow, and poverty. It was not until they experienced all of them that they realized how happy they had been in the Garden of Eden. They also realized how great the love of God who let them subdue the Garden of Eden and all things was. Just as we can see, only after we experienced the relative things and realized the true love, joy, and thanks can we love and respect God from the bottom of our hearts.

3. If you know true happiness, hope for Heaven will overflow

We have to become God's true children who obey His Word by realizing the deep love of God who placed the tree of the knowledge of good and evil. The reason why God put the tree is to let us experience the relativity and give us true happiness. Only when we realize the love of God can we win a victory with faith in any kind of difficult situation.

Those who believe God don't put hope fixed on this earth. They live only with hope for Heaven. The life on the earth is momentary, but Heaven is the eternal kingdom. We can always rejoice thinking of happiness that we will enjoy forever in the beautiful Heaven.

Affluence: Affluence is the state of having a lot of money or a high standard of living.
Spirit: things that will not die, perish, and change and that are eternal. It is life and the truth itself

- We can figure out which one is better after experiencing the one and the opposite thing to it.
It is to experience relativity. Match with the opposite thing.

Growling

Step 2

- There are many things that are opposite to each other; joy and sorrow; sickness and good health; happiness and unhappiness; etc. Look at the picture below and find out the reasons for giving thanks.

"Sally is absent today again because she is sick."

- What is the sentence below about?

To know the true value of something, you need to know the opposite thing and maybe even experience it. Adam and Eve in the Garden of Eden didn't know the true value of anything. They hadn't experienced unhappiness, so they didn't know the true happiness.

What is this?

Step 3

● Read the sentences below. When it is right, mark with O. When it is wrong, mark with X.

🏠 Adam lived in the beautiful and peaceful Garden of Eden, so he always felt happy.

🏠 Adam felt what pain, sickness, and death were like in the Garden because God taught him the knowledge of life.

🏠 Adam was sent out to the earth and realized true happiness while experiencing sorrow and pain on the earth.

🏠 Adam might or might not have eaten from the tree of the knowledge of good and evil because God gave him free will.

🏠 Unlike Adam who lived in the Garden of Eden, we have been cultivated so we know that how good the heavenly kingdom will be and we can live happily forever.

● Fill in the blanks.

God placed the tree of the knowledge of good and evil. He didn't stop Adam from eating from it when he tried eating it by his own f___ ___ ___ w___ ___ ___. It is God's providence that lets him experience all joy and sorrow. Only after experiencing r___ ___ ___ t___ ___ ___ ___ y and realizing the true love, joy, and thanks, we can love God who is love and the truth with our hearts and respect Him. That's why He allowed for the providence.

Jesus Walked on the Water

John 6:16-21

16 Now when evening came, His disciples went down to the sea,

17 and after getting into a boat, they started to cross the sea to Capernaum. It had already become dark, and Jesus had not yet come to them.

18 The sea began to be stirred up because a strong wind was blowing.

19 Then, when they had rowed about three or four miles, they saw Jesus walking on the sea and drawing near to the boat; and they were frightened.

20 But He said to them, "It is I; do not be afraid."

21 So they were willing to receive Him into the boat, and immediately the boat was at the land to which they were going.

Reading: Book of John
Lord's Footsteps

🕊 The reason why the disciples were afraid of Jesus who was walking on the water

Jesus' disciples were afraid and shouted seeing Jesus walking on the water because they thought that Jesus was a ghost. They felt scared because it was unimaginable to walk on the water. But those who live in the truth don't feel fearful. Those who keep the commandments know that God is always with them and protects them.

The Law of the Redemption of the Land

Let's Read the Bible

"The land, moreover, shall not be sold permanently, for the land is Mine; for you are but aliens and sojourners with Me. Thus for every piece of your property, you are to provide for the redemption of the land. If a fellow countryman of yours becomes so poor he has to sell part of his property, then his nearest kinsman is to come and buy back what his relative has sold." (Leviticus 25:23-25)

Let's Memorize Our Bible Verse

"Do you not know that when you present yourselves to someone as slaves for obedience, you are slaves of the one whom you obey, either of sin resulting in death, or of obedience resulting in righteousness?" (Romans 6:16)

Tradition

Have you ever heard about the Jewish tradition 'The Redemption of the Land'?

Strong Children Armed with the Word

The people of Israel have traditionally inherited the land from the father. They can't sell or buy the land they inherited. Even if they sell it because they are too poor to keep it, they can buy it again anytime they want and are able. This is the law of the redemption of the land. This law is spiritually related to our salvation. What is the relationship?

1. The spiritual law related to human salvation

God created Adam and gave him the authority to rule over the whole world. He let him rule over the fish of the sea and over the birds of the sky and over every living thing that moves on the earth (Genesis 1:28). But after Adam ate from the tree of the knowledge of good and evil by disobeying the Word of God, the situation changed. According to Romans 6:16, if men commit sins they become slaves of Satan. Adam committed sin and he ended up being a slave of Satan. And even his descendants all became sinners.

Then, how can all men be forgiven of sin and set free from the bondage under Satan? Just as each country has its own law in this world, the spiritual world also has law.

In the spiritual law, there is the punishment for sinners, "The wages of sin is death". On the contrary, there is also the law of redemption from sins. To recover the authority that Adam had to hand over to Satan, the law of the redemption from sins should be applied. This is the law of the redemption of the land.

2. The Israeli law of the redeuption redemption of the land

God didn't allow the Israelites to sell or buy their land arbitrarily. This is because all the land originally belongs to God. But if someone sells his land because he is so poor, he can recover it after becoming wealthy or his close relative can help regain it. This is the law of the redemption of the land, which is the Israelites' land law.

In other countries, once the land is sold, if the buyer doesn't want to sell it, the former owner can't help it. But the law in Israel is different. Even if the buyer of the land does not want to sell it, he has to return the land when a close relative of the original owner pays the price of the land.

3. The law of human salvation through Jesus Christ

Then, what does the law of the redemption of the land have to do with the salvation of human beings? In this law of the redemption of the land is presented the way for the salvation of the mankind who became sinners. Here, men can be likened to the land because men were created of dust from the ground (Genesis 3:19).

God said the land shall not be sold permanently, for the land is His. In the same way, men were created of dust by God and they are God's, So they shall not be sold permanently. That is, if there is a qualified man to buy back the mankind who were sold to the enemy devil, they must be given back to God. In other words, if there is a man who is eligible to recover the authority that was handed over to Satan, Satan must give all the authority back to him.

Even before the ages, God prepared the One who is qualified to take back mankind who became slaves to the devil and to regain the authority which the devil took away from Adam the first man. This is Jesus. As the time came, God sent Jesus to Israel and had Him take our burden of sins on our behalf. By doing so, He opened the way of salvation in which anyone can reach salvation with faith.

Tradition: A tradition is a custom or belief that has existed for a long time.
To redeem: If you redeem an object that used to belong to you, you get it back from someone by repaying them money that you borrowed from them, after using the object as a guarantee.
To belong to somebody: to be the property of somebody; to be owned by somebody

Step 1

- God led us to the way of salvation through the law of the redemption of the land in Israel.
  Connect the number and complete the map of Israel.

Step 2

- Just as we have the law in this world the spiritual world also has the law. Fill in the blanks.

  Law: Punishment for sinners

  The wages of ☐ is ☐.
  (Romans 6:23)
  By Adam's disobedience, all mankind became sinners and came to fall into eternal death.

  Law: Redemption from sins

  The Law of the ☐

  to regain the authority which Adam handed over to Satan due to his sin, the spiritual law redeeming men from sins should be applied.

- Find out the verse in the Bible and fill in the blanks.

  "Do you not know that when you present yourselves to someone as ☐ for obedience, you are slaves of the one whom you obey, either of ☐ resulting in ☐, or of ☐ resulting in ☐?"

  (Romans 6:16)

Step 3

- Compare the way of salvation with the law of the redemption of the land. Fill in the blanks.

The law of the redemption of the land in Israel	The way of salvation
All land belongs to _____ so it can't be sold or bought as men want.	Dust from the ground spiritually symbolizes _____
What if a poor man sold his land?	What if Satan had the authority to rule over the whole world by the sin of disobedience of Adam?
A close _____ can recover it.	Only the One who is qualified as the Savior can regain the authority. _____

- How are the law of the redemption of the land in Israel and our salvation related?

  The law of the redemption of the land is to recover men who were destined to the way of death due to sin and make them walk the way of _____ .

Jesus Promised to Send the Holy Spirit

John 7:37-39

Reading: Book of John
Lord's Footsteps

37 Now on the last day, the great day of the feast, Jesus stood and cried out, saying, "If anyone is thirsty, let him come to Me and drink.

38 He who believes in Me, as the Scripture said, 'From his innermost being will flow rivers of living water.'"

39 But this He spoke of the Spirit, whom those who believed in Him were to receive; for the Spirit was not yet given, because Jesus was not yet glorified.

Rivers of Living Water and the Holy Spirit

The 'Rivers of Living Water' means the Holy Spirit which is a gift given to those who believe Jesus Christ. When we accept Jesus as our Savior and receive the Holy Spirit, we can enjoy peace in Jesus Christ. As much as our hearts resemble the Lord's by the help of the Holy Spirit, we can pursue peace with all men and follow only goodness and love. In this way, when we become men full of the Holy Spirit we can live an abundant and happy life just like the overflowing river of living water.

A Mystery That Has Been Hidden Since Before the Ages

Let's Read the Bible

"But we speak God's wisdom in a mystery, the hidden wisdom which God predestined before the ages to our glory". (1 Corinthians 2:7)

Let's Memorize Our Bible Verse

"For the word of the cross is foolishness to those who are perishing, but to us who are being saved it is the power of God." (1 Corinthians 1:18)

Mystery

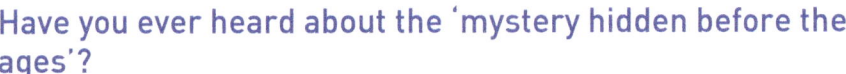

Have you ever heard about the 'mystery hidden before the ages'?

Strong Children Armed with the Word

If you understand God's providence in human cultivation, you can realize the love of God embedded in it. In addition, when we understand why He sent Jesus to the earth, we can't help giving thanks for His love and admiring His wisdom.

1. What is the mystery that has been hidden before the ages?

Even before creating men, God planned the human cultivation and came to exist as God the Trinity; God the Father, God the Son, and God the Holy Spirit. He foreknew that Adam would sin, so He already made a plan to save all men before the ages. But if the enemy devil and Satan had known it, the plan for human salvation might have failed. That's why He concealed it as a mystery.

God prepared for the way of salvation for human before the ages. When the appointed time came, He sent His only begotten Son Jesus to the earth. The God of love allowed the sinless Jesus to be crucified for our sins on our behalf. Just as the Bible says, "The wages of sin is death", we who were sinners were supposed to undergo the punishment of death, but Jesus who was sinless received the punishment on our behalf.

But Jesus had no sin at all, so He could overcome death and become resurrected on the third day from the death. Finally, He became our Savior. By this, anyone who believes Jesus Christ can be forgiven of all sins and reach salvation. This is 'the message of the cross'.

2. The enemy devil and Satan violated the spiritual law

The enemy devil thought he would be able to rule over the world as long as he killed Jesus who is God's Son. Then, how excited he was when he crucified Jesus! But here was God's mysterious providence hidden in it.

The spiritual law says, "The wages of sin is death". It also means those who haven't sinned can't see death. But the devil crucified Jesus who had no sin and no spot at all, which violated the spiritual law. In the end, he came to be unable to

control those who believe Jesus Christ as his slaves because he violated the law. In this way, Satan fell into its own trap and rather helped accomplish the providence of human salvation.

3. Through Jesus who died on the cross, the way of salvation was opened.

Adam had no choice but to go the way of eternal destruction after having committed the sin of disobedience. But the way of salvation was opened by Jesus' crucifixion and His paying the price for our sins. The enemy Satan now can't control anyone who accepts Jesus as the Savior and believes His name. Believers came to be saved and gain the right to become God's children and possess eternal life and Heaven.

1 Corinthians 2:8 reads, "The wisdom which none of the rulers of this age has understood; for if they had understood it they would not have crucified the Lord of glory." What if the enemy Satan had known the mystery before it happened? He would have disturbed the plan lest people receive salvation and wouldn't have crucified Jesus. That's why God had hidden the mystery since before the ages. It is the amazing wisdom of God.

Before the ages: tremendously long ago, before the world was formed
To fail: be unable to do it or do not succeed in doing it.

Step 1

- Everything leads to its consequence. What is the result of the pictures? Follow the dots.

Step 2

• **Complete the answers to the questions below.**

❀ To resolve the problem of sins, what did God do?

He sent His only begotten Son who had no ☐☐☐ at all and

allowed Him to take the ☐☐☐☐☐ .

By doing so, He resolved all sin-related matters.

❀ What was wrong with the thoughts of the enemy devil

The enemy devil thought if he killed ☐☐☐☐☐

he would have acted like a ☐☐☐☐ forever.

❀ How did the enemy devil violate the spiritual law?

If one hasn't committed ☐☐☐ , he or she can't reach death. But

the enemy devil crucified the ☐☐☐☐☐ Jesus.

❀ Why did God completely hide the providence of human salvation?

If the enemy devil had known the way of human ☐☐☐

☐☐☐☐☐ , he wouldn't have crucified Jesus lest

people can receive ☐☐☐☐☐☐☐☐☐ .

Step 3

● **Match the right verses.**

1 Corinthians 2:8 •
    • But we speak of God's wisdom as a mystery, the hidden wisdom which God predestined before the ages to our glory.

Romans 5:18 •
    • For the word of the cross is foolishness to those who are perishing, but to us who are being saved it is the power of God.

1 Corinthians 2:7 •
    • The wisdom which none of the rulers of this age has understood; for if they had understood it they would not have crucified the Lord of glory.

1 Corinthians 1:18 •
    • So then as through one transgression there resulted condemnation to all men, even so through one act of righteousness there resulted justification of life to all men.

Romans 5:19 •
    • For as through the one man's disobedience the many were made sinners, even so through the obedience of the One the many will be made righteous.

Jesus Forgave a Woman who Committed Adultery

John 8:4-9

4 They said to Him, "Teacher, this woman has been caught in adultery, in the very act.
5 Now in the Law Moses commanded us to stone such women; what then do You say?"
6 They were saying this, testing Him, so that they might have grounds for accusing Him. But Jesus

stooped down and with His finger wrote on the ground.

7 But when they persisted in asking Him, He straightened up, and said to them, "He who is without sin among you, let him be the first to throw a stone at her."

8 Again He stooped down and wrote on the ground.

9 When they heard it, they began to go out one by one, beginning with the older ones, and He was left alone, and the woman, where she was, in the center of the court.

What did Jesus write on the ground?

Jesus knew every sin that men secretly committed. He wrote on the ground the sins the people there had committed as if He saw all of them. Jesus didn't reveal their sins with spoken words and just wrote them on the ground. Then, the people had a qualm of conscience and left the place with shame.

Qualifications of the Savior

Let's Read the Bible

"For the word of the cross is foolishness to those who are perishing, but to us who are being saved it is the power of God." (1 Corinthians 1:18)

Let's Memorize Our Bible Verse

"And there is salvation in no one else; for there is no other name under heaven that has been given among men by which we must be saved." (Acts 4:12)

Qualifications

What kind of qualifications do you need to become a judge?

Strong Children Armed with the Word

To become a wonderful judge, you must study hard. You need to study various kinds of law and pass the bar exam. Likewise, to become the Savior who saves all mankind, the candidate needs to be eligible for the duty. Not everyone can redeem men from sins. Then, what kind of qualifications should a Savior meet? Why is Jesus qualified as the Savior?

1. He must be a man

Due to the sin of the first man, Adam, all men became sinners. So, a Savior should be a man like Adam. We've learned a close relative can recover the land in Israel according to the law of the redemption of the land. As applied in the law, only men like Adam can help men to recover the authority that Adam had handed over to the enemy devil.

Jesus is God's Son, but He came to the earth with flesh and bones like us. So He got hungry when He didn't eat. He also had to sleep. Like this, Jesus came to the earth in the form of man. So Jesus met the first qualification as the Savior–He was a man.

2. He must not be Adam's descendant

All of you were born because your father and mother got married and gave birth to you. Your father was born to his parents. Your mother was born to her parents. Following the family tree up from father to the 'greatest grand-father', you will find the first man, Adam. All of us are Adam's descendants. There is no one who can redeem us from sins among the descendants of Adam who sinned. This is because all of them have inherited sinful nature and have original sins. Sinners can't redeem others from sins.

Then, is Jesus Adam's descendant? No, He is not. He was not conceived the way we were conceived. It is not that He was born to His parents. He just borrowed the womb of Virgin Mary and He was conceived by the power of God, namely, the Holy Spirit.

3. He must have strength to win the enemy devil and Satan

To protect your brother or your friend from bad people, you need strength. Likewise, to regain Adam's authority that was taken away by Satan, strength is necessary. In the spiritual world, having no sin means having strength. Jesus was conceived by the Holy Spirit so He had no original sin. Also, He didn't commit any sin during His whole life. Since His childhood, He kept all the Word of God and obeyed God's will until He died on the cross. So He had enough strength to win over the enemy devil and Satan.

4. He must have love that can even sacrifice his life

No matter how strong you are, if you don't love your brother or your friend, you will not try to protect them. In the same manner, if the sinless Jesus hadn't loved us He wouldn't have been crucified for us. How could He have endured the pain of the crucifixion if He had had no love for us! But Jesus loved us so much so He died on the cross with joy to redeem us from our sins.

It is only Jesus who meets all the qualifications of the Savior. That's why no one can receive salvation but through Jesus Christ.

Family tree: a chart that shows all the people in a family over many generations and their relationship to one another.
Original sin: sinful nature with which one is born and that is inherited from parents

Step 1

- **Thinking of the love of the Lord who is our Savior, make a paper cross with colored-paper.**

  Preparations Colored-paper, adhesive tape or stick-type school glue

  ① Fold a colored-paper into the three equal parts.
  ② Like the picture below, fold the paper following the dotted line.
  ③ Make one more and fold them overlapping each other.
  ④ Make five more squares by doing 1 to 3 and connect them.
     The paper cross completed!

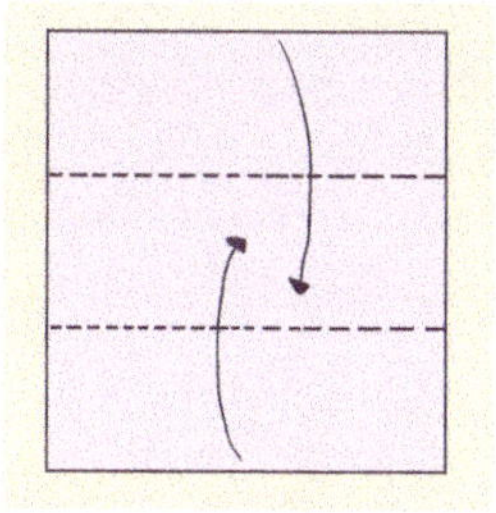

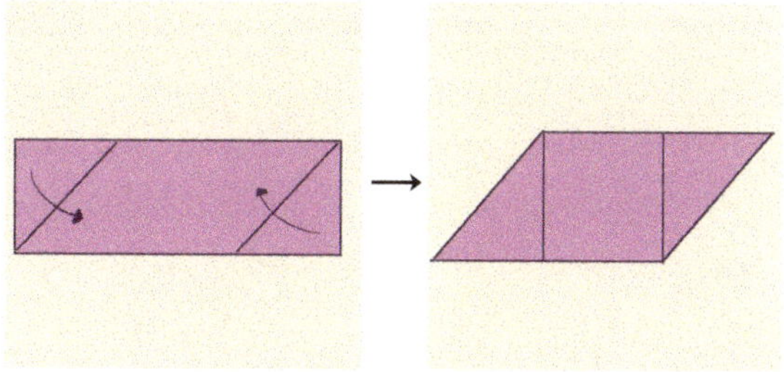

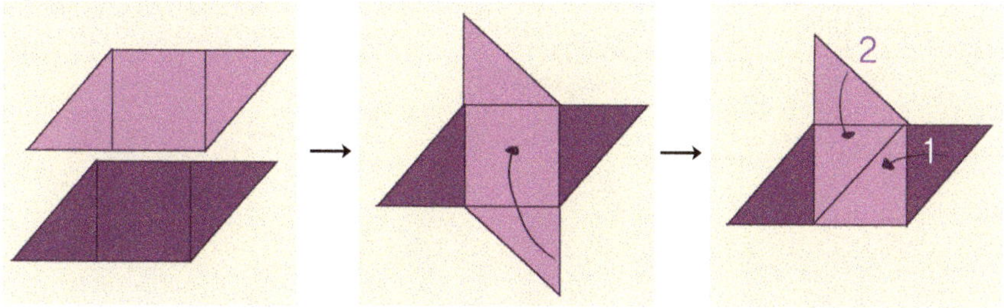

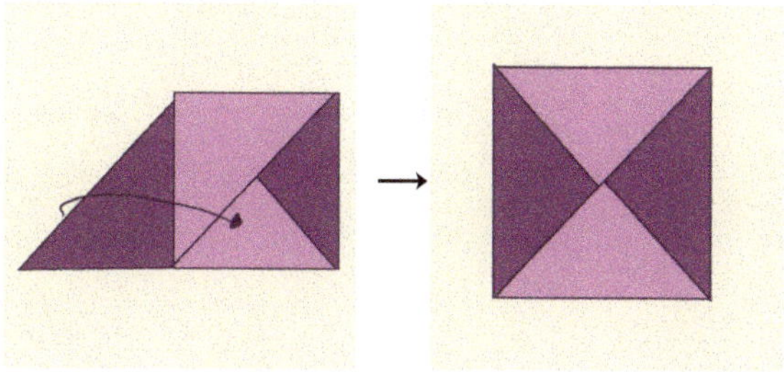

Step 2

- Write down the four qualifications of the Savior.

- Find and write down Acts 4:12.

Step 3

● Choose the true/correct sentences.

> A qualified man as the Savior must be
> a man like Adam.
>
> Jesus is not a man
> because He is the Son of God.
>
> Jesus came to the earth in flesh
> with bones like a man.
>
> Because Jesus is the Son of God,
> He didn't feel pain on the cross.
>
> Being sinless is the power
> in the spiritual world.

● What is the second qualification of the Savior?
  Why does Jesus satisfy the qualification?

Jesus Healed a Blind Man

John 9:2-7

2 And His disciples asked Him, "Rabbi, who sinned, this man or his parents, that he would be born blind?"

3 Jesus answered, "It was neither that this man sinned, nor his parents; but it was so that the works of God might be displayed in him.

4 We must work the works of Him who sent Me as long as it is day; night is coming when no one can work.

5 While I am in the world, I am the Light of the world."

6 When He had said this, He spat on the ground, and made clay of the spittle, and applied the clay to his eyes,

Reading: Book of John
Lord's Footsteps

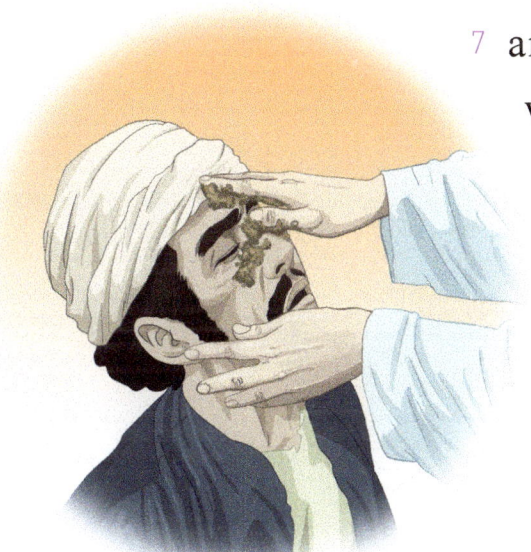

7 and said to him, "Go, wash in the pool of Siloam" (which is translated, Sent). So he went away and washed, and came back seeing."

The Reasons Why Jesus Made Clay and Applied It to the Eyes of the Blind Man

Some people believe when they just hear about God. Others believe only when they witness visible proofs. Most people believe when there is a proof, so Jesus spat on the ground, made clay of the spittle, and applied the clay to the man who was born blind. When something touched his eyes, it was easy for him to believe he would be healed and see. That's why he made clay and applied it. He helped him have faith and obey.

Jesus and Jesus Christ

Let's Read the Bible

"For this reason also, God highly exalted Him, and bestowed on Him the name which is above every name, so that at the name of Jesus every knee will bow, of those who are in heaven and on earth and under the earth, and that every tongue will confess that Jesus Christ is Lord, to the glory of God the Father." (Philippians 2:9-11)

Let's Memorize Our Bible Verse

"She will bear a Son; and you shall call His name Jesus, for He will save His people from their sins." (Matthew 1:21)

The Meanings of the Names

Do you know the meanings that the names 'Jesus' and 'Jesus Christ' carry?

Strong Children Armed with the Word

After the Lord's resurrection and ascension, His disciples received the Holy Spirit and boldly preached the gospel. They preached that there is no other name but Jesus Christ by which we must be saved. Then, what is the spiritual meaning of the name of Jesus?

1. The difference of Jesus and Jesus Christ

Just each of our names has its own meaning, the name of 'Jesus' also has meaning. Jesus is the One who will save His people from their sins. In other words, the name 'Jesus' means the One who will be crucified on the cross, will shed blood, and will save us in the future. Meanwhile, the Christ means the 'anointed one' and refers to the One who has already obtained the qualifications of the Savior.

Jesus was conceived by the Holy Spirit in God's providence and came to the earth in flesh. And He was crucified to redeem us from our sins and on the third day He was resurrected. By doing so, He became the Savior. In other words, He became the Christ who had already 'fulfilled God's providence of salvation'.

Therefore, the title 'Jesus' is used for the time He had not yet taken the cross. To refer to the time after He was crucified, overcame death, and resurrected, we have to say 'Jesus Christ' or 'Lord Jesus' or 'Lord'.

2. The difference between praying in the name of 'Jesus' and 'Jesus Christ'

If you pray in the name of Jesus Christ knowing the providence of salvation exactly, you can have a completely different power of prayer than just to pray in the name of Jesus. The title 'Jesus' is the name used before He fulfilled the providence of salvation, but the name 'Jesus Christ' contains His precious blood that redeemed us from sins, the shattering of the authority of the enemy devil that holds death, and the path to eternal life. Thus, the enemy devil and Satan are afraid of the name 'Jesus Christ' and they tremble out of fear for the name.

Depending on what name we use, God's work and answer will be different. Let me take the case of a policeman and a thief for example. If a policeman doesn't know the man next to him is a thief, the thief isn't afraid of the policeman even if he sits next to him. But if another policeman, who knows the man is a thief, appears, the thief feels afraid and runs away from him.

In the same manner, if we clearly understand the different meanings of 'Jesus' and 'Jesus Christ' and use it properly in our prayers, the enemy devil and Satan will tremble feeling fearful. Thus, we must pray or drive away the enemy devil and Satan in the name of Jesus Christ or the Lord Jesus.

3. For God's love and Jesus Christ's love, we give thanks

When God, who is love itself, saw His only begotten Son Jesus crucified, how painful it was for Him. Jesus was crucified not because of His own sins. It was because He wanted to lead all men to the way of salvation by taking the cross for our sins. God loves us so much, so He gave His only begotten Son for us and had Him take the cross on our behalf.

Therefore, we must engrave deep in our hearts the love of God who sent His only begotten Son to save us who were on the way to Hell and the love of Jesus Christ who was crucified on our behalf and opened the way of salvation. By doing so, we must always give thanks to Him.

To save: Jesus saved mankind by taking their sins on the cross
Precious blood: the blood that Jesus shed on the cross to redeem men from sins

- Read the friend's prayer and correct the wrong parts.

Beloved Lord!
Thank You for taking
the cross and saving me.
Let me achieve a white-heart
and love God all the more.
In the name of
Jesus I pray, Amen.

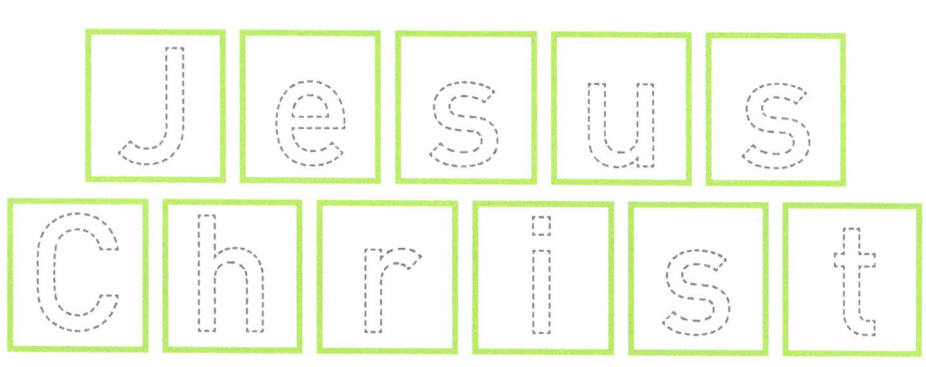

Step 2

- What do the names of Jesus who is the Savior mean?

Before the crucifixion

After the resurrection

The meaning included in the name

The meaning included in the name

- Why do we have to pray in the name of Jesus Christ or the Lord Jesus, not in the name of Jesus while praying or driving away the enemy devil and Satan?

Step 3

● Fill in the blanks using the examples.

> **Examples** Christ, Jesus, God, Holy Spirit, Jesus Christ, Lord

☐ is the One who will save His people from their sins

☐ means the 'anointed one'.

It refers to the One who has already obtained the qualification of the Savior.

We can also call 'the Lord Jesus' ☐ , Savior, and Messiah.

Thus, we should pray in the name of ☐ .

● Using the Bible, write down Matthew 1:21.

Jesus is the Good Shepherd

John 10:11-15

¹¹ I am the good shepherd; the good shepherd lays down His life for the sheep.

Reading: Book of John
Lord's Footsteps

12 He who is a hired hand, and not a shepherd, who is not the owner of the sheep, sees the wolf coming, and leaves the sheep and flees, and the wolf snatches them and scatters them.

13 He flees because he is a hired hand and is not concerned about the sheep.

14 I am the good shepherd, and I know My own and My own know Me, even as the Father knows Me and I know the Father; and I lay down My life for the sheep.

Good Shepherd and Hired Shepherds

David fought with lions or bears to protect his flock. The good shepherd protects his flock with his life, but evil shepherds, or hired shepherds, seek only their own benefits and flee when their own lives are threatened. Jesus likened us to flock. And Jesus gave His life to save us like the good shepherd.

Homework

Month

New Jerusalem Campaign

Checklist \ Date	1	2	3	4	5	6	7	8	9	10	11	12
1. Do not watch TV that offers worldly pleasure												
2. Do not use computer inappropriately or for worldly pleasure												
3. Do keep the company of friends of the opposite sex												
4. Use honorific and polite language and expressions												
5. Keep your prayer time												
Read the Bible												
6. Memorize the Bible verse												
Read Senior Pastor's books												
7. Become united as one with the shepherd												

daily check

13	14	15	16	17	18	19	20	21	22	23	24	25	26	27	28	29	30	31

Homework

Month

New Jerusalem Campaign

Checklist / Date	1	2	3	4	5	6	7	8	9	10	11	12
1. Do not watch TV that offers worldly pleasure												
2. Do not use computer inappropriately or for worldly pleasure												
3. Do keep the company of friends of the opposite sex												
4. Use honorific and polite language and expressions												
5. Keep your prayer time												
6. Read the Bible												
Memorize the Bible verse												
Read Senior Pastor's books												
7. Become united as one with the shepherd												

daily check

13	14	15	16	17	18	19	20	21	22	23	24	25	26	27	28	29	30	31

Homework

Month ◯

New Jerusalem Campaign

Checklist / Date		1	2	3	4	5	6	7	8	9	10	11	12
1	Do not watch TV that offers worldly pleasure												
2	Do not use computer inappropriately or for worldly pleasure												
3	Do keep the company of friends of the opposite sex												
4	Use honorific and polite language and expressions												
5	Keep your prayer time												
6	Read the Bible												
6	Memorize the Bible verse												
6	Read Senior Pastor's books												
7	Become united as one with the shepherd												

daily check

13	14	15	16	17	18	19	20	21	22	23	24	25	26	27	28	29	30	31

Homework

Month

New Jerusalem Campaign

Checklist / Date	1	2	3	4	5	6	7	8	9	10	11	12
1 Do not watch TV that offers worldly pleasure												
2 Do not use computer inappropriately or for worldly pleasure												
3 Do keep the company of friends of the opposite sex												
4 Use honorific and polite language and expressions												
5 Keep your prayer time												
6 Read the Bible												
6 Memorize the Bible verse												
6 Read Senior Pastor's books												
7 Become united as one with the shepherd												

daily check

13	14	15	16	17	18	19	20	21	22	23	24	25	26	27	28	29	30	31

MEMO

MEMO

The Message of the Cross
Vol. 1

Mystery Hidden before the Ages

The Message of the Cross by Dr. Jaerock Lee
Published by Urim Books (Representative: Seongnam Vin)
73, Yeouidaebang-ro 22-gil, Dongjak-gu, Seoul, Korea
www.urimbooks.com

All rights reserved. This book or parts thereof may not be reproduced in any form, stored in a retrieval system, or transmitted in any form or by any means, electronic, mechanical, photocopying, recording or otherwise, without prior written permission of the publisher.

Unless otherwise noted, all Scripture quotations are taken from the Holy Bible, NEW AMERICAN STANDARD BIBLE, ®, Copyright © 1960, 1962, 1963, 1968, 1971, 1972, 1973, 1975, 1977, 1995 by The Lockman Foundation. Used by permission.

Copyright © 2018 by Dr. Jaerock Lee
ISBN: 979-11-263-0454-7, ISBN: 979-11-263-0453-0(set)
Translation Copyright © 2014 by Dr. Esther K Chung. Used by permission.

First Edition July 2018

Previously published in Korean in 2012 by Urim Books in Seoul, Korea

Edited by Dr. Geumsun Vin
Designed by Design Team of Urim Books
Printed by Prione Printing
For more information contact: urimbook@hotmail.com

www.ingramcontent.com/pod-product-compliance
Lightning Source LLC
LaVergne TN
LVHW072124060526
838201LV00069B/4966